## Dent Wildlife Books

JOHN ANDREWS

# ADAPTABLE BIRDS

### Illustrated by
## TERRY RILEY

**J. M. Dent & Sons Ltd**

London Melbourne

# Contents

# 1 The First Birds

When the first birds were learning to fly, giant dinosaurs still roamed the earth. They were not much like the birds we see today. They looked more like feathery lizards, with teeth instead of beaks and with the clawed toes of their front feet sticking out of their wings. Nor could they fly as strongly as modern birds but were able only to glide close to the ground, or perhaps from tree to tree.

It is easy to see that birds evolved from lizard-like reptiles. But, strange as it may seem, those reptiles did not develop feathers in order to be able to fly; they did so to keep warm. Unlike birds, reptiles are cold-blooded, which means they must bask in the sun, soaking up its heat in order to be sufficiently active to hunt or to breed. Birds are warm-blooded, using some of the energy provided by their food to keep active by day or night, winter and summer. Their coat of feathers helps birds to retain their body heat, and so the first birds had a great advantage: they could hunt when reptiles were forced to seek shelter, and they could live in much colder climates.

The ability to fly came later. Perhaps when these new creatures hurried across the ground or jumped through the branches, the feathers on their front legs caused them to glide a little. That meant they could go slightly faster and further than other creatures in pursuit of prey or when fleeing from hunters. The birds that flew best would get more to

*150 million years ago the magpie-sized Archaeopteryx glided through forest glades.*

eat and live longer; they would produce more offspring like themselves. So, over many generations, spanning thousands or even millions of years, the ability to fly would have evolved.

Fossil remains of the earliest known gliding birds, called Archaeopteryx, have been found in rocks about 150 million years old. It may have taken another 50 million years for birds to develop the equipment to fly properly. The fossil skeleton of Ichthyornis, which lived about 100 million years ago, shows that, instead of having a flexible spine like Archaeopteryx, the bones of its body had already become rigidly fixed together. They formed a strong frame to support powerful flight muscles so that Ichthyornis could fly for long distances even against gusting winds – conditions which would have made Archaeopteryx lose control and crash. Another important difference was that Ichthyornis had a proper beak instead of a toothed jaw. As birds have no teeth they chew up their food with a special internal organ called a crop. Whereas a heavy jaw would unbalance a bird in flight, a crop does not.

By the time that Ichthyornis had evolved birds were spreading throughout the world, their travel made easy by the power of flight. As they settled in different habitats they evolved in different ways. Long

*Unable to fly, the dodo became extinct when man arrived in Mauritius where it had lived since prehistoric times.*

*Living in the unchanging Amazon forests, the hoatzin has evolved little over millions of years.*

before man appeared on earth, many of the kinds of birds we see today already existed. Sixty million years ago there were herons fishing by the water margin and ducks dabbling in the marshes. Hawks hunted through the forests by day and, at night, the owls took their place.

Evolution is a very slow process. It happens because every individual is slightly different from all others. Those which are best equipped for the habitat they live in will survive best. They will have the largest families and pass on their good qualities to the next generation. Those which are less suited to the habitat will produce less young and eventually die out. The shapes and skills of all living creatures have been developed in this way, fitting each kind to its own special way of life.

Some birds seem to have changed little down the ages, probably because the habitat they live in has not changed. Even today, in the Amazon forests, the chicks of the hoatzin are born with claws on their wings, rather like those of the long-extinct Archaeopteryx. These help them to clamber through the branches before they are old enough to fly.

Because evolution is so lengthy a process, creatures cannot quickly adapt to new conditions. Sudden change may bring disaster, as it did to the dodo. In distant prehistoric times, the dodo's ancestors flew to the remote island of Mauritius in the Indian Ocean. There they found abundant food in the forest where there were no predators to hunt them. Flying soon became a waste of energy. Indeed, birds which flew might have been blown out to sea and lost. So, through evolution, their wings slowly became smaller, until they were useless. Then, in the seventeenth century, seamen arrived on the island and found the dodos a welcome source of food, as did the pigs and dogs they brought with them. Unable to fly, the dodos could not escape and were soon extinct.

No doubt since birds first appeared on earth, many kinds have flourished and disappeared. Today, there are over 8,000 different species in the world. Some have simply changed into new species, evolving in a slowly changing habitat. Others died out entirely when conditions suddenly became unsuitable for them. Between them all, birds occupy a wider range of habitats than any other group of creatures, from tropical forests to polar ice-floes and from the air above mountain peaks to far below the surface of the oceans.

# 2 Equipped for Survival

In the wild, every day is a battle for survival. Each bird must find enough food for itself and, in springtime, for its growing family; the slow and the weak soon starve. Most birds are hunted by others, stronger and quicker than themselves – a moment's careless action can bring sudden death. Because of this, birds have become specialists. Each species lives in a different way from every other species and this reduces the competition between them for food, shelter and nesting places.

Keen eyesight is vital to all birds. Those which are hunted need all-round vision to reduce the risk of surprise attack, so their eyes are placed at the sides of their heads. By contrast, birds which are hunters usually have both eyes facing forwards so that they can strike accurately with taloned feet or sharp beaks when grasping their prey. Birds of prey have developed extraordinary powers of sight. An eagle can spot a rabbit in a field well over a kilometre away. Owls have evolved eyes specially adapted to seeing in the darkness so they can fly safely through woodlands at night. Their hearing is also incredibly keen: they can pinpoint the faintest sounds, and so catch mice even when it is too dark to see them. All birds of prey have strong feet with needle-sharp talons to kill their victims quickly, as well as sharply hooked beaks to tear up their prey into chunks small enough to gulp down.

*Superbly adapted for life in the water, the black-throated diver moves awkwardly on land.*

Many kinds of birds have taken to the water for food or for safety and their feet have become webbed to make efficient paddles. Some live almost entirely afloat; their short, powerful legs are placed near the rear of the body, like a ship's propellors, to drive them rapidly across the surface. Because of this, birds such as divers can move on land only by shuffling awkwardly along and resting on their chests. By contrast, geese divide their time between land and water. At night they roost afloat where foxes and other ground predators cannot sneak up on them. By day they feed on land and so they need to be able to walk easily and their legs are placed centrally under their bodies.

Some birds which swim do not have webbed feet. The coot has lobed toes instead, but it seems to manage to swim and dive quite well. It may evolve webbed feet eventually, or perhaps lobed toes are a better, more 'modern' development. Moorhens feed mainly on land: their long, flexible toes support them on marshy ground and make it possible to dash quickly to the water for safety if it is necessary. However, they do not swim as well as coots, progressing only slowly and jerkily.

Birds which live in the same way often develop the same sort of adaptations. For instance, many unrelated species have evolved long legs because they wade in shallow water or through long grass. But though they may share one habitat, the competition for food forces the

*Great white heron, roseate spoonbill, jabiru, boatbill and scarlet ibises (from left) share the same habitat but are adapted to find their food in different ways.*

*Brazilian swallowtail, sicklebill, swordbill, tawny-bellied hermit and rubythroat (from top) are all hummingbirds; their variously shaped beaks equip them to feed on the nectar of different flowers.*

*Birds' feet are adapted for many purposes, including perching (crow, top), swimming (coot, left), and running (moorhen, right).*

different species to eat different things. Gradually, birds have evolved special beak shapes ideally suited for procuring their special foods. Herons and jabirus have strong, pointed bills to grip wriggling frogs and fish. Spoonbills swing their broad-ended beaks to and fro under the water's surface to capture small creatures such as shrimps. Ibises probe the mud for worms and shellfish. Boatbills scoop up fish, frogs and shellfish in the shallows. By feeding in different ways, numerous different species of bird can live side by side.

The many kinds of hummingbird that live in tropical America almost all feed on nectar sipped from flowers but competition between them is limited because they cannot all feed from the same sort of blossoms. Each species has a different shaped beak – long or short, straight or curved – to fit different shaped flowers, like keys in locks. In turn, the flowers rely on the hummers to carry pollen from one to another and so fertilise their seeds. This sort of relationship, in which different living things depend on each other for their survival, is called symbiosis.

Essential as all these adaptations are, most birds depend above all on one special skill, the ability to fly.

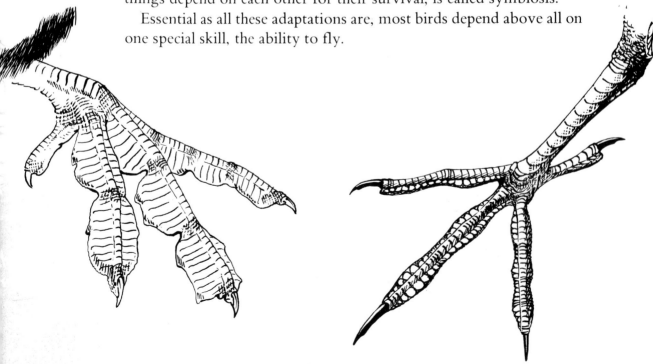

# 3 Flight and Migration

Being able to fly gives birds many advantages. Perhaps most importantly, they can quickly travel long distances to find good feeding grounds and they can easily avoid most predators. But not all birds fly in the same way. Different species have different skills, depending on where and how they live.

To sip nectar from a tropical flower, a hummingbird must be able to hover with its wings beating eighty times a second. It must fly backwards to free its long beak from the bloom or even turn a back-somersault before it zooms away. This sort of flying uses a lot of energy so hummers need to feed busily almost all day long in order to keep alive.

At the other extreme, eagles and vultures have evolved a way of flying which requires no energy at all. Their huge, broad wings will catch any rising air current so that they can soar into the sky with hardly a single wingbeat, wheeling in circles to scan the ground below for food. If hunting is bad they can live for several days at a time without feeding.

Some birds can alter the way they fly according to their needs. One such versatile flyer is the swallow-tailed kite. It can hover to watch the ground for small prey, it can fly fast or, spreading its long forked tail like an extra wing, it can slow down to weave in accurate pursuit of a

*The swallow-tailed kite is an agile hunter of small mammals and insects.*

swerving beetle. Though swallows are much smaller birds than swallow-tailed kites, and are not related to them at all, they have similar flying abilities. This is because they, too, live by catching insects in flight. They even drink from ponds on the wing.

Swallows are famed as migrants. They follow the sun to breed in the northern hemisphere while it is summer there and then wing south, escaping the cold weather when their insect food becomes scarce. Birds are almost the only creatures which can exploit the abundant food to be found during summer in the tundra lands around the Arctic Circle. Millions of wildfowl and wading birds fly north to breed there, and as summer ends move southwards to find unfrozen waters where they can winter.

Before their marathon journeys, birds must feed well, perhaps almost doubling their normal weight with reserves of fat which they use in flight, rather as a plane consumes fuel. Every year, many birds fail to complete their hazardous migrations, dying exhausted in the desert or at sea. But it does not matter that some individuals die, provided that enough survive to carry on the species.

How birds find their way across unfamiliar land and sea was for long a mystery. Now it is known that many species use the position of the sun by day and the stars by night to guide them. Some may also be able to detect the earth's magnetic field and so fly with a 'built-in compass'. Once they get close to home, their memory of the landscape enables birds to return to the very same places where they lived before – places which they know from experience will provide enough food in winter or be suitable for raising a family in summer.

*Swallows migrate from Europe to Africa in winter, returning each spring to the same nesting place.*

*Estuaries are important feeding and wintering places for waders and wildfowl including (from top) pink-footed geese, knot, dunlin and whimbrel.*

# 4 Courtship and Display

It is not enough for birds simply to find food and stay alive. They must also produce young to grow up and breed in their turn – a complicated and a dangerous business.

First, both males and females moult their old feathers, which have become frayed and worn, and grow a fresh set. In many species, the male has a special breeding plumage, brightly coloured to attract the female. Usually the female is drab by comparison so that she is less easy to see when sitting on the nest.

The male must find a territory which contains a suitable place for a nest. Birds such as gulls which breed in colonies hold tiny territories, each nesting just out of pecking distance of its neighbour. All the birds from the colony forage for food on the land and sea around them. By contrast, birds like robins hold feeding territories – each male defending an area big enough to provide food for himself and his future family. Large or small, the territory must be defended and each male bird will sing or display to warn off other males. However, it is very rare for two males to fight each other. Usually one of them backs down and leaves without too much fuss. But when the female arrives, she behaves differently and offers no challenge to the male. He accepts her in his territory and soon begins his courtship, bringing her presents of food and preening her feathers. Then the two birds mate and prepare to nest.

*Male black grouse gather at a 'lek' to display,*
*hoping to attract a mate.*

In a few species, such as black grouse, a group of males will gather at a special site called a lek and display to each other. Though they do not fight seriously, one bird becomes dominant and the others give way to it until it holds the centre of the arena. The hens visit the lek and the dominant bird mates with most of them. Then they leave, to nest and rear their broods without male help.

Some birds have developed extremely elaborate and complicated displays – none more so than the bower birds and birds of paradise. The bower birds of Australasia are quite drab to look at, so they build courts or houses, like stage sets, on which to perform and attract a mate. Some species pile up twigs round a sapling so as to form a sort of wigwam with an entrance at one side. The structure may be quite big – perhaps a metre across and over a metre high. In front of the wigwam is a 'garden' where the bird clears the ground of growing plants and then carefully covers it with moss. On the moss it places a collection of brightly coloured objects – flowers, fruit and insects. When a female visits the bower, the male sings and displays to her, perhaps carrying some colourful object such as a berry or a snail shell in its beak at the same time.

*The male bower bird builds an elaborate 'stage' on which to court its mate.*

The satin bower bird of Australia builds a smaller bower – two short lines of upright sticks making an avenue about ten centimetres wide. Often the sticks arch over to form a roof. The bower stands in a clear space which is decorated with anything coloured blue – feathers, flowers, berries, beads and bits of glass or paper. The male must protect his bower from rivals which will try to sneak in, steal his ornaments and, if possible, break down his stick avenue. He only leaves it to feed and, sometimes, to try some stealing and wrecking at his neighbours' bowers.

Bower birds are related to the birds of paradise which also display in special arenas. However, because they have brilliant plumage all they need as a stage is a branch lit by a sunbeam striking through a gap in the forest leaves overhead. Here the bird stands in the spotlight to dance, each day carefully plucking away any new leaves so as to keep the sunlit gap open. The blue bird of paradise is not content to display like the others. It actually hangs upside down with its brilliant plumes cascading around it, then it swings itself to and fro, singing as it swings.

Whatever method each species chooses for its display, the purpose is the same. It ensures that weak or nervous males do not win mates. Only the stronger, healthier birds can breed, so passing on their strength and vigour to the next generation.

*The keel-billed toucan's gaudy beak may help it to win a mate.*

*The red and blue birds of paradise are found only in the forests of New Guinea.*

# 5 The Nest and Breeding

Once the two birds have mated, they must seek a safe place for the female to lay her eggs.

Some species build no nests at all. A pair of guillemots will lay their single egg on a bare cliff ledge. The egg is wide at one end and pointed at the other so that it will not roll straight, thus reducing the risk of its falling over the edge. By nesting on cliffs, the birds find safety from ground predators and by crowding together in huge colonies they give each other protection against predatory birds such as skuas and gulls which will snatch unguarded eggs or chicks.

Many wading birds make only the simplest of nests, merely scraping a hollow in the ground in which to place their eggs. All ground-nesting birds rely on camouflage for safety from predators. Their eggs are mottled and spotted to blend with the ground itself. The parent birds too are usually plumaged in brown and grey so that they are very hard to see while sitting on the nest. Once the chicks hatch, however, they cannot stay in the same place because the movements of the adults, visiting them with food, would soon be spotted by a sharp-eyed predator, perhaps a magpie or stoat. So the chicks emerge from their eggs clad in a coat of warm, camouflaged down and are quickly led away from the nest by their parents. Though the youngsters can already feed themselves, the adults stay with them to give warmth, shelter and protection. Should an enemy approach, the chicks crouch down and 'freeze' while their parents try to distract it. Some birds will even

*The guillemot's egg is pear-shaped to prevent it from rolling off the nesting-ledge.*

*High in the branches, the magpie's domed
nest is safe from most predators.*

pretend to be injured, fluttering and tumbling over the ground to lure
the hunter away before returning to their charges.

By contrast, a bird like the magpie has much less need of
concealment. Its nest is placed high in a tree, amongst the outer
branches where few animals can climb. Over the nest cup the birds
build a dome of thorny twigs, making it difficult for predators to get at
the eggs inside. Magpies make little attempt to conceal themselves as
they go to and fro – relying on the security of the nest and on their own
bold attacks to deter marauding squirrels or crows.

Like other birds that nest above the ground, magpie chicks are born
blind, naked and helpless. The adults must bring them food and keep
the nest clean by carrying away the chicks' droppings, which are
produced neatly enclosed in a tough covering so that they are not
messy. After a few days, the chicks' eyes open and they begin to grow
feathers, but they do not leave the nest until they are able to fly and fend
for themselves. Only then will they grow their long tails – there is no
room for those in the crowded treetop home!

*The goldcrest's nest of moss, feathers and spiders' webs
is hard to see amongst the pine needles.*

Many small birds build beautifully woven nests which are often cleverly concealed. The goldcrest lays its tiny eggs in a delicate nest of soft mosses and feathers, bound together with gossamer from spiders' webs and suspended beneath a leafy branch, usually in a fir tree, where it is virtually hidden. African and Asian weaver birds thread and knot grasses together with great skill, to form a hollow ball hanging from the end of a twig. The entrance hole is at the bottom so that, though it is easily seen, it is almost impossible for a predator to get in. For added safety, weavers often suspend their nests over water, and sometimes they will choose a site close to a nest of bees or wasps which can be relied on to attack any large creature unwisely venturing too near.

Few of the young birds produced each year survive the dangers of the wild to reach maturity and breed themselves. The important thing is that there should be enough survivors to keep up the total population. In some species, the adults are long-lived, reaching an age of twenty years or more. They need lay only one or two eggs a year. In other species, like titmice, adults rarely live more than two years so they must produce a lot of eggs – perhaps ten or twelve in a clutch and two clutches each summer – if sufficient chicks are to reach breeding age.

A male black-headed weaver builds
its nest where even tree
snakes cannot climb.

# 6  Birds of the Oceans

Oceans cover two-thirds of the earth's surface and the fish and plankton which live in them offer rich pickings for birds. Habitats in the oceans are not as varied as habitats on land so there are fewer ways in which birds can use the sea. This means that there are fewer species of seabirds than of land birds. However, the marine habitats are very large so that many seabird species occur in great numbers and are very widespread – the Wilson's petrel is perhaps the most numerous bird in the world.

Spending much time on and under the water, seabirds usually have a thick layer of fat under the skin to help insulate them from cold and a particularly dense plumage to keep them dry. Few seabirds are brightly coloured – many have white underparts as this makes it harder for fish to spot them from below, and dark upperparts which help conceal them from predators flying overhead.

Several kinds of seabird fish by flying above the surface and diving after their prey. Terns normally take only small fish and stay near the shore but gannets and boobies travel far out to sea searching for larger prizes. When one bird finds a shoal and starts fishing, others soon notice and a flock quickly gathers, wheeling and diving busily. As they plummet beak first into the water, they fold back their wings like huge darts. They have specially strong skulls to absorb the impact of diving. After a few moments under water, they bob to the surface and gulp down their catch.

*The ocean-wandering shearwater (centre) may fall prey to great black-backed gulls when it comes ashore to breed.*

While gannets and terns only fish near the surface, many other species pursue their prey into the depths. Here their webbed feet are not powerful enough to propel them really fast, so many of them use their wings, which are short and stubby like flippers. Despite this, razorbills and similar birds fly quite adequately, whirring rapidly along just above the surface of the water. Penguins, though, have abandoned flight altogether, and their wings have evolved into such efficient flippers that they swim and dive superbly. Some species have grown very large: emperor penguins stand over 1 metre tall and weigh about 40kg, with a thick layer of blubber under their skins to keep out the cold of the icy Antarctic Ocean. They can swim at up to 65kph and dive to 250 metres below the surface, holding their breath for as long as twenty minutes.

But being large has its disadvantages. It takes several months for young emperor penguins to grow big enough to look after themselves and this forces the adults to start their breeding in the autumn. By the time they have finished their courtship and the female has laid her egg,

*The cormorant dives for larger fish while the razorbill (centre) and terns (right) hunt small fish near the surface.*

the winter ice has started to spread, increasing the distance to the open sea. As the female must feed to replace the stored energy which she used in making the egg, she sets off on the long walk back to open water. The male remains, balancing their egg on his feet and squatting down to wrap it warmly in his feathers. As winter blizzards howl around them, the males huddle together in groups to keep warm. At last the eggs hatch and the females return, bearing food for the chicks. Then it is the males' turn to go to sea and feed for the first time in four whole months, replenishing the fat reserves on which they have been living. Now the ice is beginning to melt again, bringing the feeding grounds slowly nearer. By midsummer the young birds are full-grown and can be left to fend for themselves when food is at its most plentiful.

Smaller seabirds can complete their breeding in a few weeks but they have to face other dangers. A number of species exist by robbing and killing their neighbours. Great black-backed gulls can easily kill an adult shearwater so that these birds, and some others, nest in burrows for safety, taking the added precaution of coming and going only by night when the gulls are roosting. Frigate birds are pirates, harrying

*Insulated by a thick layer of blubber, emperor penguins rear their chicks in icy Antarctica.*

*Frigate birds, boobies and tropic
birds (top to centre) inhabit
the tropical oceans. The male
frigate has a balloon-like throat
pouch which it inflates
when displaying to a female.*

terns until they drop the fish they are carrying to their own chicks. The frigate is, in fact, quite able to fish for itself – and does so with such skill that it snatches fish from the water without wetting its plumage.

Fish and plankton shoals move with the seasons, and so many seabirds have to travel great distances in pursuit each year. Among the best adapted for this are the albatrosses, which feed on squid in the Pacific and south Atlantic. Here the winds blow almost ceaselessly and albatrosses take advantage of these conditions. They have evolved extremely long, narrow wings which they simply hold out stiffly and so glide swiftly along. By altering the angle of their wings and wheeling round to face the wind, they soar aloft and from there begin another effortless ride downwind. This system of flying is called 'dynamic soaring' since it uses very little of the birds' energy. The wandering albatross, which may reach an age of fifty or more, has a greater wingspan than any other bird, stretching 3.5 metres from tip to tip.

It is clear that birds have made a great success of their colonisation of the world's oceans. They have become well adapted to flourish amid ice, wind and waves.

*The wandering albatross dwarfs two Wilson's petrels picking plankton from the wavetops.*

# 7 Birds of the Wetlands

From mountain torrents to sluggish rivers, from lakes and ponds to marshes and mudflats, wetlands have been colonised by a great variety of birds. Unlike the oceans, many wetlands contain a diversity of plants on which birds can feed, as well as copious animal life in the water and the mud.

One of the best known waterbirds is the kingfisher, renowned for its skill in diving to catch fish. Yet many kinds of kingfishers live only on dry land, catching lizards and insects. It is easy to imagine how once, long ago, a kingfisher saw a small fish in a pool and mistook it for some kind of lizard. It would have had an unexpected wetting but discovered a new and successful way of hunting.

It is harder to guess how some other waterbirds learned to fish. The skimmer, for instance, flies along just above the water with its beak open and the lower mandible sticking down just below the surface. As soon as it touches a fish, the skimmer flips its victim out of the water and swallows it.

Birds which feed on the seeds and leaves of plants must have first ventured into water when reaching for some lush growth near the edge. Now they have evolved many different ways of using the habitat. Swans have developed long necks to reach waterweeds growing well below the surface. Geese normally feed on land, preferring to graze on grass, though they like to roost afloat at night for safety from predators. Some ducks dive to obtain their food. For example, pochard seek underwater plants, while tufted ducks eat insects and water snails. Mergansers have beaks with serrated edges to enable them to grip fish.

*A kingfisher will dive for fish, while skimmers snap them from the surface.*

Other ducks feed only from the surface; the pintail takes plant and insect food. It often upends but never dives. The drake pintail is bigger than the female and has a longer reach, which means that when food is short in winter it can feed in deeper water than the female and need not share the same scarce food supply.

A late-comer to the wetlands is the dipper. It has not yet evolved special adaptations for life under water but simply walks along the beds of streams, gripping stones with its feet to stop itself being washed away as it searches for insect larvae and small snails. Because dippers are small they can find enough food to live on in small streams where there is insufficient for ducks.

There are many tiny creatures, as well as algae – minute plants – to be found in water or mud. Several species of birds have developed filters in their beaks to sift out this food. The huge beak of the flamingo is just such a device. By waggling its tongue to and fro the bird pumps water through fine sieves inside its bill to trap great quantities of midge larvae, tiny shrimps and algae. Clearly the food resource is a rich one as flamingos grow to 1.5 metres tall, breeding in colonies which may contain tens of thousands of birds.

Like wildfowl, many different kinds of waders have evolved to exploit different conditions. Curlews use their long, curved beaks to extract ragworms from their tunnels in the sand and mud of the seashore. Snipe have straight beaks to probe for earthworms in inland marshes. Both have long-toed feet to support them as they walk over soft ground. Phalaropes are related to the other waders but have

*White-fronted geese feed mainly on grass while the merganser (swimming) feeds on fish.*

Flamingos sieve tiny plants and animals from the mud and water of salt lakes.

abandoned wading for swimming. They have partly webbed feet because they feed by spinning round and round in shallow water to stir up small creatures from the bottom.

The urgent search for food lasts all year round. In cold weather, frost and ice prevent wetland birds from feeding and so they must move to milder areas. Huge flocks congregate at the coasts where they find rich feeding in the mudflats, which remain unfrozen because of the warmth of the sea. In spring the birds disperse and great numbers travel north to the tundra lands around the Arctic Circle where, for a few summer months, the pools and lakes thaw, providing abundant plant and insect food on which birds can rear their young. The Arctic summer is unreliable and in some years sudden blizzards destroy many eggs and chicks, so that the bird population declines noticeably. Then comes a good year, many chicks are reared and numbers recover.

*Snipe, curlew, red-necked phalarope and dipper (from top) all share the same habitats in summer but live on different food.*

# 8  Birds of Plains and Deserts

On the plains there is too little rainfall to support trees so only grass, wild flowers and scrub can grow. In deserts the rain is so infrequent that even grass cannot survive, though there may be oases of lush greenery where springs come to the surface. The birds that inhabit these areas have to be able to combat heat and lack of water as well as avoid predators in a landscape without cover.

Many open country birds – such as bustards, coursers, grouse and quail – prefer to run rather than fly. By crouching close to the ground or scurrying away they may escape notice, whereas taking wing would make them conspicious. The American roadrunner is only the size of a small chicken but it can race along at 30kph. Using its long tail as a balance, it dodges about with great agility, rarely needing to fly to escape danger.

However, the ability to fly well is important to most birds of the plains and deserts because places where they can drink may be few and far between. Sandgrouse will fly a 100-kilometre round-trip to find water, usually arriving at dawn or dusk to escape the attention of birds of prey which lie in wait around these areas. Sandgrouse have the unique habit of soaking their breast feathers with water to carry it back for their chicks to drink. Bathing too is a problem, yet birds must keep

*The flightless Australian emu, second only in size to the ostrich, can run at great speed to escape its enemies.*

their feathers clean and free of parasites. Many species make scrapes in the dusty soil and work it through their feathers to cleanse them.

A few plains birds have given up flight altogether and this has allowed them to grow very large in size. The biggest living bird is the ostrich. An adult male may be 2.3 metres from head to feet. Its great height and large eyes give it splendid all-round vision and make it very difficult for any large predator to approach unseen. Often ostriches flock together with grazing antelopes or zebras, sharing the look-out with them. If danger approaches, the birds can make off at over 65kph, a speed they are able to maintain over long distances. Their feet are unlike those of ordinary birds as they have only two toes, one of which is particularly large and strong for transmitting the powerful thrust of the leg muscles to the ground. Rheas in South America, emus in Australia, and ostriches in Africa live in the same sort of habitats and behave in a similar way. All three species look remarkably alike even though they are not related.

High daytime temperatures in summer mean that breeding birds try to site their nests wherever a rock or shrub gives shade. Some nest in burrows – elf owls dig their own or move into the abandoned holes of prairie dogs. However, in winter it can be very cold and many birds migrate away from the plains and deserts. The American poorwill, a kind of nightjar, is the only species of bird known to hibernate. In winter when its insect food is not available, it becomes torpid and motionless, its body temperature falls, its heartbeat slows and it lives on its stores of body fat until the hot weather returns.

Thus birds have found many ways of surviving in exposed habitats despite harsh climates and lack of shelter.

*This displaying sage grouse and the Californian quail inhabit the North American grasslands.*

*The houbara bustard (top), pin-tailed sandgrouse (centre), collared pratincole (left) and cream-coloured courser all have camouflaged plumage to blend with their surroundings.*

# 9 Birds of the Forests

South of the tundra a broad belt of conifer forest stretches around the world. Here the summer is short and the trees, which grow only during the few weeks of warm weather, cannot afford to waste hard-won energy by shedding their leaves each winter. Instead, pine, fir and spruce have waxy needles which survive the frost and snow, unlike the soft, broad leaves of deciduous trees. Though insects are plentiful in summer, food becomes very scarce in winter and only a few bird species are able to live in these forests all year round.

Some birds eat the foliage and seeds of the trees themselves. The turkey-sized capercaillie feeds on young conifer shoots. So does the grosbeak which, being a finch, is much smaller and can feed on small twigs unable to support the capercaillie's weight. Crossbills are also finches and are specially adapted to eat the seeds from fir-cones; the tips of the upper and lower mandibles of their beaks cross each other, making a tool for prising open the scales of cones to get at the seeds. Because many conifer seeds ripen in winter, the crossbills must rear

*The cock capercaillie spreads its tail in display and crows with a sound like popping corks.*

*Pied flycatcher and green woodpecker seek insects
in different parts of the same oak tree.*

their young at that time. The small chicks have to survive in air
temperatures of −35°C, which is far colder than humans could endure
without thick protective clothing.

Titmice feed on insects and spiders, killing more than they need when
supplies are plentiful in summer and storing the surplus in bark crevices
or amongst tufts of pine needles. When winter comes and they must
search long for every morsel of food, they chance upon their hidden
stores and these help them to survive through the long months when
live insects are very scarce.

In warmer areas of the world, where winters are less hard and rainfall
is regular, deciduous forests develop. Here, trees have broad leaves, best
suited to capturing the sunlight needed for growth. Because they shed
these leaves in winter, many small plants can grow beneath them,
flowering in spring before the trees' leafy canopy opens, cutting off the
sun. There are far more insects and seeds for birds to eat in these regions
than in the northern forests.

The insect eaters have developed many ways of seeking food.
Warblers hunt along the twigs and amongst the leaves; some, like the
wood warbler, prefer the treetops while others, such as the whitethroat,
feed in bushes and shrubs. Flycatchers perch where they can see all
round and, when an insect comes within range, flit quickly out, grab it
and return to the same perch to await their next victim. Thrushes find

Left *The crowned pigeons of New Guinea are the largest pigeons in the world.*

Right *Great horned owl, quetzal (centre) — worshipped by the Aztecs — and scarlet macaw feed on the fruit of the South American forests.*

their food on the ground, turning over fallen leaves and hopping through the grass as they search for snails and worms.

The woodpecker is specially adapted to feed on those insects that live under the bark of trees or bore into the wood, which other birds cannot reach. Its sharp, strong beak is set in a specially strengthened skull mounted on a very muscular neck. The bird clings tightly to the tree, leaning back and supporting itself by pressing its stiffened tail feathers against the trunk. Then it bores rapidly into the wood with repeated blows of its beak – like a hammer drill. When it breaks into the tunnel of a wood-boring insect, the woodpecker extends a very long, thin tongue with a barbed tip, to pursue the victim down its hole and pull it out.

There are no migrants in the tropical forests. This is because conditions there remain the same all year round, without shortages to make birds move away or surpluses to attract them in. Tropical forests contain the greatest diversity of tree and plant species, in turn supporting the greatest variety of resident birds.

Many species are adapted to feed on fruit. The toucan's long beak may enable it to feed on fruit growing from twigs too thin to support its weight whereas the quetzal solves that problem by grabbing fruits in flight. Fruit pigeons have very wide gapes so they can quickly gulp

*In Africa, the crowned eagle feeds on the monkeys*
*it captures and kills in the treetops.*

down large beakfuls. Parrots eat fruit too and are agile enough to
clamber where some of their competitors cannot reach. Many of them
also have beaks strong enough to crack nuts. When the fruit of one
forest tree ripens, many sorts of birds will congregate to enjoy it and, by
flocking together, they may gain extra protection from birds of prey.
Many eyes share the watch for danger and when one gives its alarm call,
all are alerted.

Hawks, with their rounded wings and long tails, can fly fast between
forest trees in pursuit of smaller birds. Owls, active when other birds
are roosting, feed mainly on mammals. Eagles seek the larger creatures.
Despite its 2.4 metre wingspan, the South American harpy eagle can
weave through the forest at up to 80kph to capture and kill the monkeys
that live in the treetops.

From the woodland floor, up the trunks of the trees, along the
branches to the tips of new twigs and beyond that into the sky above,
birds have found a great variety of ways to harvest the rich crop of
seeds, fruit, insects and other animal life to be found in the world's
forests.

# 10 Birds of the Mountains

The tops of high mountains are as cold as the Arctic, with snow lying all year round. Below the snowline there is open rocky ground and lower still there may be grassy meadows fringed by scrub and conifer woodland. To live here, birds have to contend not only with scarcity of food, but with extreme cold and high winds.

Small birds usually avoid the wind by flying very little, preferring to keep under cover amongst the rocks and scrub. Nevertheless large species may use it to help them travel fast and far. Eagles and vultures hunt over vast areas, using rising currents of warm air or updraughts from the mountainsides to lift them high into the sky, whence they glide great distances. Largest of all birds of prey is the Andean condor, a South American vulture with broad wings 3 metres long that give it maximum lift on rising air. Vultures feed only on carrion; their feet are too weak and short-clawed to kill live prey. Eagles will take carrion if they find it but are well able to hunt and kill for themselves.

Owls take only live prey. One species, the snowy owl, is adapted to live in the extreme conditions of the Arctic and also on mountains in northern Europe and America. Its white plumage helps camouflage it against the snow and a dense coat of feathers covers not only its body but also its beak, legs and toes, giving excellent protection against the cold.

Falcons also hunt in the open highlands where their speed of flight comes into its own. A peregrine falcon will sit on a high crag or circle far overhead until a crow or pigeon comes within range. Then it will take off in swift flight to dive down on its prey at speeds well over 160kph,

*The Andean condor, heaviest of all flying birds, feeds only on carrion.*

*The snowy owl's dense white
plumage is ideal for life in the
high Arctic and on northern mountains.*

striking so hard with its talons that the victim may be killed instantly. But falcons are not always successful in their hunting. The intended prey may see the danger in time to dive for cover amongst the rocks, or it may successfully dodge the hunter in mid air. Choughs are particularly adept at manoeuvring in flight and, like ravens to which they are related, seem to enjoy swooping and soaring around the rock-faces where they nest. Very social birds, choughs often feed and fly in groups; perhaps this makes it harder for a bird of prey to approach unseen.

Because of the lack of plant life, most mountain birds feed on other creatures, including invertebrates such as insects, worms and spiders. Choughs use their curved beaks to probe the alpine turf for ants and other insects. The rock-faces themselves provide a feeding place for wallcreepers which hop up the sheer surface like woodpeckers, poking in crevices for spiders and other small prey. Several kinds of pheasants scratch over the stony ground with strong feet, digging vigorously for roots, bulbs, worms and grubs. Dotterel pick insects and other small creatures off the surface of the ground.

Unlike most birds, it is the male dotterel which incubates the eggs and this may be because food is so scarce on the mountaintop that the female cannot store enough body fat both to make the eggs and tide her over the incubation period. Instead, having laid the eggs, she must feed

A selection of birds from the mountains of
Europe: (from top) Alpine swift, peregrine
falcon, alpine chough, wallcreeper and dotterel.

*The Himalayan blood pheasant lives at altitudes of up to 4,500 metres.*

herself up while the male takes over. Because of this, his plumage is less brightly coloured than hers, aiding concealment on the open ground.

In the air above the mountains, alpine swifts catch insects at speeds of over 160kph. Swifts are designed for life in flight. Their legs are so short that they cannot perch normally, or walk, but must nest on crags or buildings where they can fly straight into the nest site. Remarkably, it is only when swifts are nesting that they ever come to earth. At dusk they wheel up to great altitudes, passing the night on the wing. An adult feeding chicks may fly several hundred kilometres each day, returning from each foray with its throat packed full of insects.

Birds have come a very long way from the distant prehistoric days when they learned to glide in the sheltered forest glades. Their modern descendants have evolved many different ways of flying so that they are even able to ride high winds and storms in the thin air above snow-capped mountain peaks.

# 11 Conservation

Through the millions of years since they first appeared in the world, birds have continued to evolve, changing slightly from one generation to the next so that they have gradually adapted to a multitude of conditions and habitats. Many species have disappeared because they evolved into something more suited to their environment, as did Archaeopteryx. A few have become extinct, like the dodo, when faced by sudden change to which they could not quickly adapt.

Now the world is changing faster than ever before. The habitats of many birds are disappearing too rapidly for them to adapt to others. Great areas of the northern conifer forests have been felled to provide man with timber for buildings and wood pulp to make paper. Most of the broad-leaved forests in temperate lands have been cleared to make farmland and now the tropical forests are being cut for timber and to open up land for rapidly increasing human populations. Vast areas of the American prairies and the Asian steppes have been ploughed to grow wheat, while in Africa the savannah grasslands slowly shrink in area. In many estuaries, seaports and polluting industries have destroyed the rich mudflats and marshes. Inland, the wetlands are drained for farming or to prevent flooding.

At sea, the fishing fleets of many nations compete for smaller and smaller numbers of fish. This means that there are less for seabirds to

*The famous avocet is a rare bird that owes its survival in Britain to nature reserves; it is used as the symbol of the Royal Society for the Protection of Birds.*

eat. In some parts of the world's oceans, frequent oil pollution regularly kills large numbers of birds. On islands, the introduction by man of dogs, cats, rats, pigs and other creatures has resulted in the extinction of many flightless species and caused a great decline in the numbers of seabirds which nest on the ground.

In countries all over the world millions of birds are deliberately killed each year, for food or for sport, and many more are trapped to be kept in cages. Some species, especially birds of prey, are destroyed because they are assumed to compete with man for the animals and birds which he farms or hunts.

It is true that some species have benefited from the changes. For instance, those that are adapted to the conditions which man creates on farmland have done well. Larks nest in the open fields and finches breed in the hedgerows. But even farms are less suitable for birds than they once were, mainly because the use of chemicals to kill weeds and insects removes their food supply.

The need for conservation is great. Even in countries where there are good laws to protect birds, areas of natural habitat grow less every year.

Fortunately, all over the world, people are beginning to realise that action must be taken quickly to protect wildlife and the beauty of nature from the great dangers presented by an ever-increasing population and the modern industrial world. Some countries have passed laws which prevent people from killing birds or taking their eggs. More and more nations are learning the importance of trying to prevent pollution. To protect the habitats of rare species, nature reserves are being set up where the land is managed specially for wildlife.

All of us can help conserve the natural world. When we visit the countryside, we should take care not to damage or disturb wildlife. We can support conservation societies by joining them, and give practical help by carrying out wildlife surveys or working on reserves in our spare time. We can encourage other people to help too.

There is a lot to be done and time is running out for many rare birds. It is up to us all to save them.